Jesus Talk To Me

Jesus, Talk To Me

How To Get God's Attention

Sermon In A Book
Vol. 1

First Edition

Copyright ©2017 Ken McDonald
All rights reserved.

ISBN: 978-1-942769-01-9

No part of this book may be used or reproduced in any manner whatsoever without written permission except in case of brief quotations embodied in critical articles and
reviews.

All Scripture quotes are from the
Authorized Version of 1611.

Designed by Ken and Terri Lee McDonald
Cover photo used by permission from
www.shutterstock.com

www.kenmcdonaldfamily.com

Other Books By Ken McDonald B.D., Th.M.

Here Comes The Bride
A critique of the Baptist Bride Heresy

Pursuit
One Man's Quest to Find God's Perfect Will for His Life

Defiled
The Spiritual Dangers of Alternative Medicine

Dealing With Bad In-Laws
A Bible study on Jacob and Laban
(Sermon in a Book Series, Vol. 2)

Even As God
Healing Relationships Biblically
(Sermon in a Book Series, Vol. 3)

Good Vibrations
Overcoming Spasmodic Dysphonia through vocal behavior exercises

Table of Contents

Introduction..11

1. Herod..25

2. Pilate..35

3. The Dying Thief...................................45

4. Emmaus Road....................................55

Introduction

Warm air blew the little girls' hair out of her eyes as the door opened to the fast food restaurant. The familiar smell of maple, hot coffee, toasted egg muffins; sausage and bacon made her realize how hungry she was. Her mother had her by the hand and pulled her aside as a group of five or six uniformed Little League baseball players came out the door heading to practice on this Saturday morning. After the Little Leaguers quickly filed by them, grabbing little Emily's hand a bit tighter, her mom pulled her into the restaurant.

Though familiar to both of them, for they had eaten many a meal there, this morning they did not go up and order a meal. Instead Emily's mother led her to a booth on the far side of the

Jesus, Talk To Me

restaurant and made her sit down. Mother seemed short and agitated this morning. Emily could tell something was different. She knew that from the very start of the day when her mother came into her bedroom. It was earlier than usual that Emily's mom came into her bedroom and got her out of bed. She then rushed out of the house with little Emily who was still dressed in her pajamas and not even combing her hair. She said they were late and had to hurry.

There were many other people coming and going in the restaurant that morning. Laughter arose from a table not far away, while at other tables people sat and ate quietly as if in deep thought, but probably more than likely just waking up and getting going.

The "tiger" in little Emily's tummy seemed to be growling, so she spoke up and asked, "Mommy, can we get something to eat?"

"No!" was the quick and semi-harsh reply. "He can pay for it!"

"Who can pay for it, mommy?" was the little girl's reply.

"I didn't want you to be troubled so I didn't tell you, but you are going to see your father today," was the mothers' reply.

Surprise, and fear mixed with excitement and uncertainty, all at once came into the little girl's heart.

As a question she replied, "I'm going to see Daddy today?"

Introduction

She briefly thought of how she was dressed, pajamas and how her hair wasn't even combed, but the thought soon left as memories of daddy flooded her mind.

She remembered the last time that she saw him. She was standing on her bed, looking out the window screaming and crying as she watched the police put him in the back seat of the patrol car and take him away. She remembered crying and wondering if she would ever see him again. She thought of the many days alone in her room, and drawing pictures for Daddy. She remembered how she had tried to write letters to him telling how she missed him and would sign it, 'Love, Emily". Would he ever read them? Would they ever get to him? Discouraged by her mother, she left them in a drawer in hopes that someday, maybe . . . and then she would not think about it anymore.

As if awakened out of sleep, the quick look of her mother brought Emily back into reality as she saw her look towards the door behind her. Emily could tell daddy was here. As she began to turn around to see him, he was already by Emily's side, but looking at Sarah, her mother.

Sarah stood up with her eyes glancing to him and then away, seemingly in a panic of where to look and not knowing what to do. Then in a brief stern voice she gave a short, "Hi, Carl."

Dad was a harsh man and they had been through many a fight. The air seemed to fill with tension when Carl spoke in a way that Emily had

Jesus, Talk To Me

never heard him speak before.

"Hi, Sarah, it's good to see you."

"Oh, really? I bet it..."

Emily heard her mother speak and fear gripped her again as it had before when she could tell a fight was going to begin, but it was different today.

Carl spoke up, stopping her before she could say much more, by saying with his familiar gruff voice, yet now in a tender sort of way, "Sarah, I'm sorry. Would you please forgive me?"

These words disarmed Sarah, Emily's mother, for a split second and then not knowing what to say she blurted out, "I've got to go."

Carl replied, again tenderly, "Please stay."

Emily watched her mom again seemingly disarmed and in a way confused.

Sarah thought, "This wasn't like Carl." This wasn't the gruff, cussing jerk that she had known a year ago. She thought he must have been putting on a good act, yet his sincerity betrayed the thought.

"No, I've got to go," was her reply as she nervously and quickly turned to leave.

A few people from other tables glanced up when they heard the conversation.

His eyes followed her all the way to the door as she left, and for a moment, which to little Emily seemed like an eternity, he stood there with his back to her.

Fear, excitement and wonder all gripped her as he started to turn around to look at his girl. As

Introduction

she sat on that booth bench looking upward, to where he stood, and to Emily he seemed like the tallest building in the entire city. It seemed he was so tall, as tall as a giant, and she so small, as just a little thing.

Emily tried to speak, but the fear and emotion gripped her so that the only thing that came out was a soft and timid, "Daddy."

Was he angry? His face seemed still as he beheld her. She wondered if he was even glad to see her, even though she was so glad to see him.

Then he did something that little Emily would never forget. He didn't sit down, but standing by the side of the table he bent his knees and came down to her level. Then looking into her eyes he softly said, "Emily...my little girl, my little princess." She saw some tears fill her Daddy's eyes, as he said to her, "I have missed you so much! Thank you, Lord Jesus, for this time with Emily. Thank you for answering prayer."

She had never heard him mention Jesus before, except when he was mad. Then as she began to say, "I've missed you too" he reached out and took her in his strong arms and picked her up with a hug that she never had before from Daddy. He hugged her, and she put her tender, little arms around his neck and hugged him too. Then she heard him say, "I love you so much."

"I love you too, Daddy" Emily replied, and then she noticed as she glanced across the restaurant, that Sarah had stopped outside. Carl's back was

Jesus, Talk To Me

to the window, but Emily was facing the window and through it Emily saw that she was watching Daddy and her. Sarah wiped a tear from her eye and then saw Emily was looking so she walked on to the car.

"Are you hungry?" he asked. With this question, the months apart melted away into a forgotten memory.

"Yes, Daddy, I am very hungry, and Daddy, I have a lot of letters that I wrote to you, but they are at the house in my bedroom." Her innocent, tender words touched his ears and played a melody that only a father can know.

His arms held her firm and strong, and she noticed he was listening to all that she had to say. She told him what she liked to eat, that she had other clothes at home, still feeling bad she wasn't dressed up for him. Little Emily talked and talked to him. This was her Daddy, and he was listening to all that she had to say. Emily had his attention and it meant so much to her.

What a joy it is when someone we love or look up to pays us some attention! Has there ever been someone in your life that you looked up to, such as a teacher, a pastor, mother, father, or a friend?

Usually, but not always, those whom we highly respect are older than we are. Perhaps they gave us instruction, advice, love, or helped solve a problem in our life, and what a joy it is when they pay some attention to us. What a joy it is when we have the opportunity to talk to them, and they in

Introduction

turn talk to us.

I remember when I was traveling to a preaching meeting. We had started out from Memphis, TN, and I drove for a few hours. As I drove, my right ear began to hurt more and more. After five hours of driving, I had my wife, Terri, "take the wheel" as my ear was hurting so badly it was distracting me from driving. She drove for a few hours, and all the while the pain in my ear was growing worse and worse.

Terri asked if I wanted to go to an emergency room. Not having insurance I replied, "No, I will be alright." By now I was beginning to shake, my head was tilted to one side a bit, and my eyes were closed. Another hour went by and Terri said, "I am taking you to the emergency room." I merely replied, "OK."

We checked in, and Terri did the talking and arranging for the doctor to see me. I did not pay much attention to the formalities of registration. After an hour of waiting, we were allowed to enter into a patient examination room. A nurse entered and took my pulse, temperature and a few other basic determinations for the doctor to have some information about me. I did not care about what the nurse was doing, nor did I pay her much attention.

Another painful forty-five minutes went by, and finally the doctor came into the room to examine me. When I knew it was the doctor, I opened my eyes, greeted him, and was really glad he was

17

attending to me. Finally I had a doctor's attention. This excited me; because I knew he could prescribe some pain medication as well as whatever else I needed to get over the ear infection. By then the infection had my ear canal so swollen it was closed shut.

Has there ever been someone you looked up to, and you wanted to get their attention? What a joy it is, or what a relief it is when they are in your presence and pay some attention to you.

Maybe you are confused about an issue, or issues in your life. Maybe there is an instructor, or a pastor that you would like to confide in and ask them your questions. Within you there is an expectant hope that they will give you the answers to your questions that would clear up your confusion. Their advice would make your life better, and the direction you are going much more clear.

The moment comes, and all other matters of your life are pushed out of your thoughts as you have the opportunity to talk to them and to ask them your questions. Even more of a joy is when they respond to you. You can tell they listened to you, thought about your questions and you are now getting a reply from them.

With eagerness you listen, intent on what they tell you. You concentrate and make sure you intellectually digest what they are saying. While at the same time there is an excitement as you realize that they are paying some attention to you.

Introduction

In life there are those we look up to, those who have answers for our dilemmas, and those who give us answers to the questions that come into our lives. Yet, how much greater it is when we get our Lord Jesus Christ's attention!

You know that Jesus Christ has all the answers to all of your questions. Some may say, "Well, it's all in the word of God. The word of God has all the answers." Yes, but there are those personal decisions and times of life that you need a direct, personal reply from the Lord Jesus Christ. That time when you need personal direction for your life. The Lord may use a verse or verses from the word of God, which is fine, because the word of God is the only thing you can trust.

The question arises though-how do you get the Lord's attention? No, I am not saying you will hear a voice, or receive a sign, both of which cannot be fully trusted. But you may receive a direct answer to prayer, or have some verses stand out to you in a personal way whereby you know the Lord himself is speaking to you.

But, how do you get the Lord's attention?

You know He has the answer to any question you have. You know that Jesus Christ can solve any problem you have, to that there is no doubt. You know that the Lord is able to do exceeding abundantly above all that we can ask or think. He can solve your problem, but how do you get the Lord's attention?

Let me qualify this again. No, you are never out

of the Lord's sight and He will never leave thee nor forsake thee, praise the Lord! You are never alone, and no, he is never too busy for you, but how do you get His attention? How do you get him to answer your questions and remove your confusion?

I remember when I arrived at Bible school in Pensacola, Florida. The year was 1979, and I was twenty years old. I had been saved just two years earlier, with no religious background of any kind. Green as grass, I was beginning Bible school, for I knew that I had been called to preach and that my Lord had led me to that Bible school.

As I started classes there was a mixture of married and single students. I was single. Along with that there was a mixture of students from the North, South, and a few others, such as myself, were from the West. Some students grew up in church; others were just coming off of drugs or had just been released from prison. Some had college degrees and others had never graduated from high school; it was a very interesting mixture of people, and I was one of them.

Now and then we would have guest preachers come in for meetings, and I remember one such preacher but before I describe his preaching, let me first say that often southerners are very demonstrative. By that, I mean they get emotional and shout or even run the aisles. For them, this is normal "church". Northerners are much more stoic and straight-laced. Emotion is not expressed

Introduction

as easily for northerners, as they tend to be more mental, and think more than southerners. Westerners, we just kind of observe what's going on.

Well, here I was in one such meeting, and this southern preacher started preaching. Man, could he "shell the corn!" He could get in your row of corn and go to town. By that I mean he was a very good preacher, and was very demonstrative in his preaching. I, as a fairly-new Christian, was easily impressionable, and he certainly made an impression on me.

As he was preaching, I remember him saying that he had been in a rough time, and he needed God to hear and to answer his prayer. With a fervency, shouting as he preached, and sweat running off his face, he told the story:

"I decided that I needed to get ahold of God. I just had to get ahold of God, so I got me a bottle of water and went out in the forest and knelt down under an old, oak tree. I lifted up my voice, and said 'Oh God ah, Iah, aint ah, goin' to ah, leave here ah, unteel ah, you answa my ah, prayer ah!!'"

As I sat there, hearing that, in my California way I said to myself, "Cool!" I was impressed!

Well, a couple of years went by and I graduated from Bible school. I then headed back out west to "set the world on fire for God," but it has also been said (in an Asian sort of way), "He that go out to set the world on fire, soon come back for more

Jesus, Talk To Me

matches." That's how it was for me. Things were just not going well, and then I remembered that preacher. I remembered how he went out under the old, oak tree; knelt down, prayed, and got his prayer answered. I took inventory of things and decided that this was one of those times where I had to do something similar.

So I took a box of Kleenex and went out to my car, which was where I did most of my praying. I climbed into the car and knelt on the passenger side front seat of the Mazda GLC. I did not tell my wife or children what I was doing, I just did it.

There all by myself I began to pray. Then I began to scream, plead, cry, yell, and to request the Lord's help with great fervency. I was crying, slinging snot, and wrestling as best I knew how with my Lord Jesus Christ. This lasted about two hours. The windows fogged up, I was wringing wet, my voice was hoarse, and I had yelled all that I had to yell.

There, alone on my knees, I figured that I had done it. Yep! I had gotten ahold of God, and He was going to answer my prayers. A certain confidence swelled up in me, and I was sure that I had gotten ahold of God.

I climbed out of the car and went back into the house. As I opened the door and entered into the kitchen, Terri was there cooking. Looking at me, she asked, "Was that you?"

I asked hoarsely, "What do you mean?"

She replied, I thought I heard someone

Introduction

screaming."

I said, "Yes, that was me. I just needed to get ahold of God."

You may ask, "Did you get ahold of God, and did He answer your prayer?" Well, no, He didn't answer my prayer. I did not get His attention; at least not the way I wanted.

So, how do you get the Lord's attention?

Jesus, Talk To Me

Chapter 1

HEROD

Take your Bible and turn to Luke 23:3-9

Luke 23:3 And Pilate asked him, saying, Art thou the King of the Jews? And he answered him and said, Thou sayest it.

Luke 23:4 Then said Pilate to the chief priests and to the people, I find no fault in this man.

Luke 23:5 And they were the more fierce, saying, He stirreth up the people, teaching throughout all Jewry, beginning from Galilee to this place.

Luke 23:6 When Pilate heard of Galilee, he asked whether the man were a Galilean.

Luke 23:7 And as soon as he knew that he belonged unto Herod's jurisdiction, he sent him to Herod, who himself also was at Jerusalem at that time.

Jesus, Talk To Me

> Luke 23:8 And when Herod saw Jesus, he was exceeding glad: for he was desirous to see him of a long season, because he had heard many things of him; and he hoped to have seen some miracle done by him.
>
> Luke 23:9 Then he questioned with him in many words; but he answered him nothing.

Pilate, trying to get Jesus off his hands, sends him to Herod in verse seven. You will notice that Herod is "exceeding glad" to finally be able to see Jesus Christ. He had heard of the many things that Jesus had done, and as the scripture states, Herod was hoping to see some kind of miracle done by him. Yet, when Jesus Christ is in the presence of Herod He doesn't give him the time of day. He answers him, zip, zero, nada! Not one word from the Son of God.

Now that is not what you want the Creator of the universe to do to you! Jesus said in John 15:5 without me ye can do nothing. When you have no input into your life from the Lord Jesus Christ, you are in a mess! Wise is the one who realizes his need for the Lord Jesus Christ in his life.

In this portion of the word of God though, we have a man, Herod, who is desirous to hear from Jesus Christ, but why doesn't the Lord pay him any attention? Ah yes! This is very instructive. The reason the Creator of the universe does not give Herod any kind of an answer is because Herod had already rejected light from God.

Herod

Three and one half years earlier, Herod had another man on his hands by the name of John the Baptist. (Actually his name was John, and the Baptist part was a title attributed to him. It is not a reference to a religious denomination.) The Bible says:

> Mark 6:17 For Herod himself had sent forth and laid hold upon John, and bound him in prison for Herodias' sake, his brother Philip's wife: for he had married her.
> Mark 6:18 For John had said unto Herod, It is not lawful for thee to have thy brother's wife.
> Mark 6:19 Therefore Herodias had a quarrel against him, and would have killed him; but she could not:
> Mark 6:20 For Herod feared John, knowing that he was a just man and an holy, and observed him; and when he heard him, he did many things, and heard him gladly.

Three and a half years earlier Herod had an open heart towards the things of God, so God was showing and giving him light. Even though he had John arrested, notice in 6:20, it says that "Herod feared John." Do you notice it never says that he feared Jesus Christ? Notice in verse 20 why Herod feared John. "Knowing that he was a just man and an holy." At this point, just three and a half years earlier than in Luke 23, Herod had a reverence for the things of God.

Not only so, but it says that he observed him. Herod paid attention to John and was aware of him. It also says in verse twenty that he "heard him gladly." This is quite a statement, for John was preaching holiness and repentance from sin. John was preaching and telling Herod to repent in verse eighteen, "It is not lawful for thee to have thy brother's wife", and Herod was OK with that, for he had a respect for the things of God at this time.

Herod is getting light from God. He has God's attention, you might say, and is listening to the things of God, but he won't act on the light that he is getting from the Lord. To not accept light, or truth, is to reject it. There is no middle ground.

So Herod is placed in a position where he must take sides. His stepdaughter comes and dances for him on his birthday. It is very pleasing to him, so he tells her that she can have whatever she wants to the half of the kingdom.

> Mark 6:21 And when a convenient day was come, that Herod on his birthday made a supper to his lords, high captains, and chief estates of Galilee;
> Mark 6:22 And when the daughter of the said Herodias came in, and danced, and pleased Herod and them that sat with him, the king said unto the damsel, Ask of me whatsoever thou wilt, and I will give it thee.
> Mark 6:23 And he sware unto her, Whatsoever

Herod

thou shalt ask of me, I will give it thee, unto the half of my kingdom.

Mark 6:24 And she went forth, and said unto her mother, What shall I ask? And she said, The head of John the Baptist.

Mark 6:25 And she came in straightway with haste unto the king, and asked, saying, I will that thou give me by and by in a charger the head of John the Baptist.

Mark 6:26 And the king was exceeding sorry; yet for his oath's sake, and for their sakes which sat with him, he would not reject her.

Mark 6:27 And immediately the king sent an executioner, and commanded his head to be brought: and he went and beheaded him in the prison,

Mark 6:28 And brought his head in a charger, and gave it to the damsel: and the damsel gave it to her mother.

This is an amazing story! The young girl, his niece, runs and asks her mother what she should ask for, and the mother tells her to ask for the head of John the Baptist. Now think about that for a minute. That is a very wicked request no doubt, but watch the reaction of the girl. Mark 6:25 And she came in straightway with haste unto the king...

She asks her mother, the mother tells her to ask for the head of John the Baptist, and she returns in haste to ask for his head. There is no

Jesus, Talk To Me

incredulity, there is no hesitation, nor any astonishment. She just hurries back to ask for his head. That is a wicked mother and daughter to say the least.

So Herod is now stuck between a rock and a hard place. He gave his word, to the half of the kingdom, but he is exceeding sorry he made the promise. What could he have done?

The same question was asked of a class of young Sunday school kids and one of them replied, "Well, he could have said that wasn't in that half of the kingdom." Herod hadn't thought of that escape so he is bound.

God is going to put you in a position sooner or later whereby you are going to have to choose which way to go. You are either going to choose what's right, clean and Godly, or you are going to choose to please man. It's one or the other. Herod chooses to have John's head cut off.

Herod rejects the light that God had given him through John the Baptist. God gives light of creation and of his existence to every person that enters the world. In John 1:9 Jesus Christ is the "...true Light, which lighteth every man that cometh into the world." And in this life God gives you light. When you reject that light you don't get anymore. You determine the amount of light you receive.

So, now let's go forward three and one half years. Herod is in Jerusalem. Pilate sends Jesus Christ to him and Herod is excited at the thought of

Herod

having Jesus Christ in his presence. Was he excited because of the possibly of getting light from God for his life? No! Did Herod fear Jesus Christ, like he feared John the Baptist? No!

When you reject light, you become a bit more hardened towards the things of God and Herod is now hardened. He is not seeking light. Herod merely wants to be entertained. Luke 23:8 ...He hoped to have seen some miracle done by him. But God is not in the entertainment business.

Herod now has God manifest in the flesh, the Lord Jesus Christ, right in front of him, and God is not giving him one word. Not one single word!

> Luke 23:9 Then he questioned with him in many words; but he answered him nothing.
> Luke 23:10 And the chief priests and scribes stood and vehemently accused him.
> Luke 23:11 And Herod with his men of war set him at nought, and mocked him, and arrayed him in a gorgeous robe, and sent him again to Pilate.

In a haughty, arrogant manner, in front of everyone, perhaps Herod addresses Jesus Christ,

Herod; "So Jesus, I hear you can heal people. I've heard that you have opened the eyes and given sight to the blind. Is that true?"

With all eyes looking at the Son of God for an answer, there is stone-faced silence. Not one word."

Jesus, Talk To Me
Herod commands some men, "Slap Him."

They slap and they mock Him, yet He does not speak.

Herod again speaks up and says, "I hear that you have fed multitudes. I heard it was..." looking to his men, "Five thousand? Was it five thousand men, not counting women and children? Jesus, is that true?"

Again all eyes fasten on Jesus Christ, yet there is silence. Not a word comes from His lips.

Again, Herod commands, "Slap Him, mock Him, spit on Him."

> Isaiah 50:6 I gave my back to the smiters, and my cheeks to them that plucked off the hair: I hid not my face from shame and spitting.

Herod again mockingly says, "Hey men, are you hungry?" To which many answer, "Yes, Your Majesty, we are very hungry!" The reply comes back accented with laughter and mockery.

Herod then says to Jesus, "How about a meal, Jesus? Fix us lunch, and we'll believe on you."

Silence from the Son of God...not one single word!

God is ignoring him, because Herod has rejected the light that God had already sent him through the person of John the Baptist, as well as the fact that Herod merely wants to be entertained. When you reject light you don't get anymore.

If there was a time when God was dealing with

Herod

you about something, and now it seems like you can't get ahold of Him, or He seems so far from you, then you need to go back to where he was dealing with you before.

Obviously you can't go back in time, but if God has dealt with you about something, and you never dealt with Him about it then it is there that you will find Him. It is there that you will get His attention. Until you get it settled with Him it isn't settled at all.

If you are reading this, then it is likely you are sincere and do not have a mocking attitude. Maybe you are frustrated, scared, or discouraged. If there was a time when God was dealing with you about something, then that is where you will find Him again.

Israel had come out of Egypt by the power of God. He led them up to the Promised Land and sent spies into the land, among whom was Joshua and Caleb. (Numbers 13) All of the spies, except Joshua and Caleb, feared when they saw the giants in the land.

By the way, in the Bible, no one ever died from a giant!

When the spies came back, they discouraged the hearts of Israel, thus making Israel afraid to go into the Promised Land. For forty years Israel wandered in the wilderness and then is brought back to the very same place forty years later, and in so many words God asks them, "Are you ready now?"

Jesus, Talk To Me

Maybe there was a time in your life when God was dealing with you, and you hesitated. Perhaps out of fear. If you want his attention you are going to have to deal with Him in regards to the last place He dealt with you. The last light that you received from Him is where you will find Him again. Until then you won't get much from Jesus Christ. There will be a wall between you and Him in the sense of spiritual light and fellowship with your Saviour.

Chapter 2

PILATE

Luke 23:3 And Pilate asked him, saying, Art thou the King of the Jews? And he answered him and said, Thou sayest it.

Did you notice that the Lord spoke and paid attention to Pilate even though He wouldn't pay attention to Herod? As a matter of fact, the Lord speaks quite a bit to Pilate. Notice John 18.

John 18:33 Then Pilate entered into the judgment hall again, and called Jesus, and said unto him, Art thou the King of the Jews?
John 18:34 Jesus answered him, Sayest thou this thing of thyself, or did others tell it thee of me?
John 18:35 Pilate answered, Am I a Jew?

Jesus, Talk To Me
>Thine own nation and the chief priests have delivered thee unto me: what hast thou done?
>John 18:36 Jesus answered, My kingdom is not of this world: if my kingdom were of this world, then would my servants fight, that I should not be delivered to the Jews: but now is my kingdom not from hence.

You will notice that when Jesus Christ deals with Pilate, He answers him, but not plainly. You might say the answers are kind of veiled. Pilates asks if He is the King of the Jews and the Lord answers so as to frustrate Pilate in verse thirty-four. John 18:34 Jesus answered him, Sayest thou this thing of thyself, or did others tell it thee of me?

Then in verse thirty-six the Lord answers by saying that His kingdom is not of this world, and in verse thirty-seven He states: Pilate therefore said unto him, Art thou a king then? Jesus answered, Thou sayest that I am a king. To this end was I born, and for this cause came I into the world, that I should bear witness unto the truth. Every one that is of the truth heareth my voice.

At this time the Lord Jesus Christ pays quite a bit of attention to Pilate. This tells me that Pilate has not rejected light the way that Herod had. Pilate is honest and open, while at the same time under a great amount of stress knowing that Jesus Christ is innocent, I find in him no fault at all. (Vs. 38)

Pilate is a picture of a lost person who is getting

Pilate

light but wants to stay neutral. He doesn't want to reject the light, but it is not convenient to accept the light at this time.

Did you ever notice the story in the book of Acts?

> Acts 24:24 And after certain days, when Felix came with his wife Drusilla, which was a Jewess, he sent for Paul, and heard him concerning the faith in Christ.
> Acts 24:25 And as he reasoned of righteousness, temperance, and judgment to come, Felix trembled, and answered, Go thy way for this time; when I have a convenient season, I will call for thee.
> Acts 24:26 He hoped also that money should have been given him of Paul, that he might loose him: wherefore he sent for him the oftener, and communed with him.
> Acts 24:27 But after two years Porcius Festus came into Felix' room: and Felix, willing to shew the Jews a pleasure, left Paul bound.

Did you notice the convenient season never came? It will never be convenient to do right and to live for the Lord Jesus Christ. It will never be convenient to repent of your sins and trust Jesus Christ as your Lord and Saviour. It will never be convenient! But it is what you ought to do and the time is now! Not tomorrow, but now! It will only be harder to do right tomorrow, and it most certainly will not be convenient.

Well, back to Pilate.

Jesus, Talk To Me

John 19:5 Then came Jesus forth, wearing the crown of thorns, and the purple robe. And Pilate saith unto them, Behold the man!

John 19:6 When the chief priests therefore and officers saw him, they cried out, saying, Crucify him, crucify him. Pilate saith unto them, Take ye him, and crucify him: for I find no fault in him.

John 19:7 The Jews answered him, We have a law, and by our law he ought to die, because he made himself the Son of God.

John 19:8 When Pilate therefore heard that saying, he was the more afraid;

John 19:9 And went again into the judgment hall, and saith unto Jesus, Whence art thou? But Jesus gave him no answer.

John 19:10 Then saith Pilate unto him, Speakest thou not unto me? knowest thou not that I have power to crucify thee, and have power to release thee?

John 19:11 Jesus answered, Thou couldest have no power at all against me, except it were given thee from above: therefore he that delivered me unto thee hath the greater sin.

John 19:12 And from thenceforth Pilate sought to release him: but the Jews cried out, saying, If thou let this man go, thou art not Caesar's friend: whosoever maketh himself a king speaketh against Caesar.

Pilate

There is an interesting thing here. Pilate has been getting light from the Light of the world, Jesus Christ. Now watch the change in response from Jesus Christ towards Pilate.

Pilate knows Jesus Christ is innocent, and along with that there is a certain amount of fear growing in Him. Then, some more light, his wife sends him a note:

> Matthew 27:19 When he was set down on the judgment seat, his wife sent unto him, saying, Have thou nothing to do with that just man: for I have suffered many things this day in a dream because of him.

So his fear is growing as he tries to figure a way to release Jesus Christ. He proclaims, "I find no fault in this man." (Of course, Jesus Christ is the Lamb of God without spot and blemish. Thank you, Pilate, for making that known.) Then the chief priests cry out,

> John 19:7 The Jews answered him, We have a law, and by our law he ought to die, because he made himself the Son of God.

Pilate's heart skips a beat, and he goes back into the judgment hall to talk to Jesus.

In that hall stands a man wearing a bloodstained purple robe. He has a crown of thorns that has been beat down upon His head. Blood is running

Jesus, Talk To Me

down His legs and onto the floor. His beard has been "plucked" (Isa. 50:6) off of His cheeks, and blood is dripping off those cheeks and landing on the floor.

Pilate walks up to Him and says, John 19:9 Whence art thou?

This is not a question such as, "Are you from Bethlehem, or Nazareth?" This is an outer space question. He is asking, "Are you from Heaven?" But notice what happens. Jesus Christ does not answer him. Vs 9 ...But Jesus gave him no answer.

Jesus is starting to treat Pilate the same way that He treated Herod, which was to answer him nothing. Pilate has been given light from more than one source, and now it is time for Pilate to act on the light, but he is trying to stay neutral.

When you are around the truth--whether it be the word of God, a sermon from the word of God, or directly from the One who is the Way, the Truth, and the Life, Jesus Christ--then you must make a decision to accept or reject the truth. There is no other choice. The truth forces you to move forward or backward, but it is impossible to stay neutral when you are around the truth.

The truth requires, by its very nature, action. If you do not accept the truth then YOU ARE REJECTING IT.

A girl in her twenties wrote her father. The young lady had recently been born again and was burdened for her father. She so wanted to know

Pilate

that her father was going to Heaven when he died.

There had never been much religion of any kind in their home, so she wrote and told him of how Jesus Christ had left Heaven, was born of a virgin, lived a sinless life, and died on the cross to pay for his sins. She told him of how Jesus Christ was buried, and after three days and nights he arose from the dead--victorious over sin and the grave. She then told him how he needed to admit that he, too, had broken God's law and was therefore a sinner and needed to trust Jesus Christ as his personal Saviour.

I have condensed her story, but after some weeks she received a letter from him. In the letter he told of how he did believe in Jesus, but that he just did not need him right now, but if he ever did that she would be the first to know.

His belief was no different than the belief of devils. What he was trying to do was to stay neutral, but he didn't stay neutral, he rejected salvation.

Pilate is trying to stay neutral, but Jesus Christ is not accepting that, for Pilate in reality is rejecting the light that God has been giving him. So Jesus Christ stands there silent. No answer! All that can be heard is the sound of an angry crowd outside thirsting for blood.

> John 19:10 Then saith Pilate unto him, Speakest thou not unto me? knowest thou not that I have power to crucify thee, and have power to release thee?

Jesus, Talk To Me

> John 19:11 Jesus answered, Thou couldest have no power at all against me, except it were given thee from above: therefore he that delivered me unto thee hath the greater sin.

Now comes the last words Pilate ever hears from the Son of God, and when Jesus Christ says, "from above" he answers Pilates question. The last word Pilate hears from Jesus Christ is the word "sin."

The Lord answered his question, but when He did, it was not a plain answer. It was somewhat veiled. It was like that before I was born again. I heard truth, but I did not understand what I was hearing. I was blind and without understanding. The Lord was giving me light, and He was paying me some attention, but I just did not understand it all.

This went on for about two weeks as some friends of mine had been born again and were telling me about salvation. Finally one night I understood what I needed to do and arriving home very late that night I knelt beside my bed, prayed and asked Jesus Christ to forgive me of my sins. I confessed I was a sinner and I believed that Jesus Christ had died on the cross for me. I called on Him to come into my heart, to forgive me, and to save me. That night my destiny changed and I was born again!

When I prayed that night, I don't know what the Lord of the universe was doing. When you think about it, the fact that the God of the universe would stop and listen to me, it sort of boggles the mind. But whatever He was doing, when I knelt, prayed and said, "Dear Jesus..." I got His attention! Glory to God!

One day in the town of Jericho, just on the outskirts of the town, beside the road there sat a blind man. His name was Bartimaeus. He was sitting there begging just trying to survive. People walked by, camels, donkeys, and carts went by and the dust rose up and settled on the cloak that Bartimaeus had wrapped himself in. Bartimaeus did not ever go by, he could only sit still and beg.

On a certain day He heard the sound of a great number of people coming his way. He asked what it meant, only to have someone harshly snap at him, "It's Jesus of Nazareth, He's passing this way." Upon hearing this He said out loud, but speaking to himself, "I've heard of this man."

Bartimaeus perked up his ears, lifted his head and listened, as the crowd grew ever closer. Sitting by the roadside, he heard all the news of the day, thus he had been hearing of this man for some time. Of how he had healed lepers, and many others who were crippled and sick.

He did not know where Jesus was, for he could not see. All he could do was try to yell out above the commotion of the crowd. Mark 10:47 Jesus, thou Son of David, have mercy on me.

People began to yell at him, telling him to be quiet and to hold his peace. But the more they tried to quiet him down, the more he yelled out for

Jesus, Talk To Me

help, and the Bible says that, Jesus stood still. Bartimaeus was just a poor blind beggar, yet his cry stopped God in his tracts. He had gotten the Lord's attention.

> Mark 10:49 And Jesus stood still, and commanded him to be called. And they call the blind man, saying unto him, Be of good comfort, rise; he calleth thee.
> Mark 10:50 And he, casting away his garment, rose, and came to Jesus.
> Mark 10:51 And Jesus answered and said unto him, What wilt thou that I should do unto thee? The blind man said unto him, Lord, that I might receive my sight.
> Mark 10:52 And Jesus said unto him, Go thy way; thy faith hath made thee whole. And immediately he received his sight, and followed Jesus in the way.

Herod couldn't get one word out of Jesus Christ for Herod had rejected light three and a half years earlier. Jesus Christ did talk to Pilate, and that quite a bit, though in a way veiled and not plain, yet it was light. The Lord Jesus Christ did pay some attention to Pilate which was more than enough for Pilate to know what he should do, but he didn't do what he knew was right. It wasn't convenient!

Chapter 3

THE DYING THIEF

Now we come to another man in this study of "Jesus, Talk To Me": the dying thief.

> Matt. 27:41 Likewise also the chief priests mocking him, with the scribes and elders, said,
> Matt. 27:42 He saved others; himself he cannot save. If he be the King of Israel, let him now come down from the cross, and we will believe him.
> Matt. 27:43 He trusted in God; let him deliver him now, if he will have him: for he said, I am the Son of God.
> Matt. 27:44 The thieves also, which were crucified with him, cast the same in his teeth.

In the early hours of the crucifixion there were the chief priests, scribes, and Pharisees coming by

Jesus, Talk To Me

to mock the Lord Jesus Christ. During this time the Bible states, Matt. 27:44 The thieves also, which were crucified with him, cast the same in his teeth.

The thieves are angry, bitter and obviously in pain. Were they angry at Jesus Christ? I don't know! I see no reason for them to be angry at Him, but they were directing words of slander and mockery towards Him.

Isn't it amazing how people blame God so easily! I will never cease to be amazed at how people will blame God, or claim to be mad at God. Hello? Are you stupid? I'm going to pick a fight with God! Hello? Do you think you will win?

One of the most common reasons in this age for people to quit living for Jesus Christ, or to never get born again is that they are mad at God. In their mind they think, "I have every right to be mad at God." That is the same attitude Satan has towards God. May I remind you that, if you are not born again, then God has every right to cast you into Hell right now?

Four rugged street fighting men, half staggered and half strutted, out of the bar after closing at two in the morning. The crisp cold air blew lightly against their faces and seemed to sober them up a bit. As each one climbed on his motorcycle, one noticed his friend hold a clenched fist up in the air with his eyes looking into the starry sky.

Defiantly words were uttered--something to the effect of, "God, I defy you. Just try to deal with

The Dieing Thief

me."

His friend heard the words and saw what he did, but didn't really think too much about it. He just climbed on his motorcycle the same as the others, and the four of them kicked their motors over, and with a loud popping roar that pierced the early morning silence of the cold night, they headed out of town.

Just a few blocks into their trip and a cop car turned on his lights and siren and started pursuit. Another cop car joined in the chase.

The one who had shaken his fist at God already had four tickets just in recent weeks and if he got caught would surely be going back to jail.

At high speed two of the motorcycles broke off and one police car veered to pursue them. The other cop car stayed in pursuit of Charlie and his friend. Charlie knew that if his friend was stopped he would be going to jail, so Charlie turned off hoping the cop would come after him, but it did not work. The cop stayed in pursuit of his friend.

When it was all over Charlie found out his friend had laid his bike over and slid headfirst, straight into the corner of a cement step, split his head open and died. Less than an hour earlier he had shaken his fist at God, but had lost.

In the early hours of the crucifixion both of the dying thieves revile Jesus Christ. But as time goes by something happens to one of the thieves. Maybe he thought about hearing Jesus Christ ask forgiveness for those who were crucifying him. Or

Jesus, Talk To Me

hearing Jesus give instructions to John to take care of Mary. Whichever it was, between the hours of nine o'clock A.M. and twelve noon one of those dying thieves has a change of heart.

During that time though, Jesus Christ, who was on the cross right beside him, never gave him one word. It was the same treatment that Herod received. One of the dying thieves begins to revile Jesus Christ again only to be rebuked by the other one.

> Luke 23:39 And one of the malefactors which were hanged railed on him, saying, If thou be Christ, save thyself and us.
> Luke 23:40 But the other answering rebuked him, saying, Dost not thou fear God, seeing thou art in the same condemnation?
> Luke 23:41 And we indeed justly; for we receive the due reward of our deeds: but this man hath done nothing amiss.
> Luke 23:42 And he said unto Jesus, Lord, remember me when thou comest into thy kingdom.
> Luke 23:43 And Jesus said unto him, Verily I say unto thee, To day shalt thou be with me in paradise.

Through the hours of suffering, one of the thieves acknowledges that he is getting what he deserved. He is honest about himself. This is the first step in getting the Lord's attention. You have

The Dieing Thief

to be honest about yourself in light of the word of God. Nothing hidden, no lies, no deals, complete surrender is needed if you are going to get the attention of Jesus Christ.

In other words, you must repent, if you are going to get the Lord's attention. You must come to the Lord and acknowledge your sins, or that you are a sinner.

That is what man does not like to admit. People have the hardest time admitting they are no good. They might admit that they are fairly bad, but it is so hard for people to admit that they are no good. The Bible says there is none good and that includes me as well as you. If you want to get the Lord's attention then you must condemn yourself and justify God.

The Bible says that Jesus Christ did no sin, neither was guile found in him (1 Peter 2:22). Can you match that?

Here is the eighth commandment, Exodus 20:15 Thou shalt not steal. Have you ever stolen anything in your life? Have you ever taken anything that wasn't yours? Someone who steals is called a thief. There are two of them that died on Calvary when Jesus Christ was crucified. If you have ever stolen anything then you are a thief. Since God is holy and righteous, do you think He will let a thief into Heaven?

> 1Cor. 6:9 Know ye not that the unrighteous shall not inherit the kingdom of God? Be not

Jesus, Talk To Me

> deceived: neither fornicators, nor idolaters, nor adulterers, nor effeminate, nor abusers of themselves with mankind,
>
> 1Cor. 6:10 Nor thieves, nor covetous, nor drunkards, nor revilers, nor extortioners, shall inherit the kingdom of God.

Here is the ninth commandment, Deut. 5:20 Neither shalt thou bear false witness against thy neighbour. Have you ever told a lie? The term for someone who lies is a liar. If so, then you are a liar.

Now God is holy. Do you think God will allow lying thieves into Heaven? Here is what the Bible says:

> Rev. 21:8 But the fearful, and unbelieving, and the abominable, and murderers, and whoremongers, and sorcerers, and idolaters, and all liars, shall have their part in the lake which burneth with fire and brimstone: which is the second death.

If you are saved, then your sins are washed away by the blood of Jesus Christ (Revelation 1:5 ...Unto him that loved us, and washed us from our sins in his own blood), but are you in fellowship with your Saviour? Is there something hindering your relationship with Jesus Christ such as sin? 1John 1:9 If we confess our sins, he is faithful and just to forgive us our sins, and to cleanse us from all

The Dieing Thief

unrighteousness.

The first step in getting God's attention, whether you are saved or lost is the need for repentance. If you are saved then you need to confess your sins to your Saviour. Isn't that what the word of God says? Yes, it is!

This modern "Christianity" has very little in common with true Bible Christianity. Modern Christianity has "Christian" Rock and Roll, "Christian" Karate, "Christian" Yoga or Christoga, "Christian" witchcraft (I'm not making this up, Google it) Church in Bars, "Christian" wine and beer, as well as many other things. If you want God's attention, then you need to repent of your sins and attempt, as best you can, to live a clean life.

If you have been backslidden, or if you have just been saved, thank God for His being so gracious and forgiving as soon as you acknowledge your sins to Him. When you repent and trust Jesus Christ for your salvation, He does not hesitate. Or when you repent and come back to the open and loving arms of your Saviour, Jesus Christ, again, He does not hesitate to forgive you. Jesus Christ is good, He loves you and desires for your return to Him just as the father of the prodigal welcomed his son, but the son was repentant.

On Golgotha that day beside Jesus Christ, one of the thieves changed his view of himself. He repented and condemned himself, but then he also justified the Lord Jesus Christ, as he rightly

Jesus, Talk To Me

proclaims, Luke 23:41 This man hath done nothing amis.

When he did this, he got a direct reply from the Lord Jesus Christ. It was not veiled, or confusing like it was with Pilate, but was a straightforward, direct reply that he had absolutely no trouble understanding. When Jesus was done talking to him, he knew exactly where he was going when he died. There was no doubt about it.

When I read this story I can't help but realize that if there was ever a time when the Lord would have been too busy for someone it would have been right here on the cross. There is no doubt that Jesus Christ is in Pain. The Bible says in Psalm 22:14 I am poured out like water, and all my bones are out of joint. He is taking on the sin of the world as well as doing battle with Satan himself according to Isaiah 50:8 He is near that justifieth me; who will contend with me? let us stand together: who is mine adversary? let him come near to me. He is becoming sin for us that we might be made the righteousness of God in Him. 2 Corinthians 5:2 For he hath made him to be sin for us, who knew no sin; that we might be made the righteousness of God in him.

If there was ever a time when the Lord Jesus Christ would have been too busy for a guilty thief, this would have been the time yet in the middle of it all, a guilty thief calls out to Jesus Christ, gets the Lord's attention, and receives a direct reply from the God of the universe.

The key to that direct reply can be summed up

The Dieing Thief

in one word, repentance. The thief repented, which opened up the communication with the Lord Jesus Christ.

When is the last time you repented? How long has it been since you got alone with God and confessed your sins? How long has it been since you shed some honest tears over your sins? Isaiah 66:2b ...but to this man will I look, even to him that is poor and of a contrite spirit, and trembleth at my word. How long has it been since you have been in contrition over your sins?

At the end of the life of King Saul, God was not answering him. In so many words, God was not giving him the time of day. The reason was that when King Saul got caught, or did wrong, he justified himself. He wouldn't genuinely repent.

King David, on the other hand, was a good repenter. Consider his adultery with Bathsheba, and the murder of Uriah, as well as the numbering of Israel. Each time David repented and took the blame. Thus God was with him, paid attention to him, and dealt with him all the way to the end of his life.

It is essential, if you want to get the Lord's attention, to repent and confess your sins to the Lord Jesus Christ. This is not for salvation. Salvation takes place when you receive Jesus Christ as your personal Saviour (John 1:12, Romans 10:13) and you are born again. Salvation is a free gift that you cannot work for (Romans 5:1).

Jesus, Talk To Me

The dying thief repented and got the Lord's attention. In his case, it is a picture of salvation as a free gift because he could not do a thing to earn his salvation, he just repented and asked. That is how I got saved and that is how you will get saved if you are lost.

If you are saved, the lesson is the need for repentance in order to clear the way for fellowship with your Saviour.

I remember the night I prayed and got the Lord's attention. I don't know what He was doing, but He stopped what He was doing, reached way down and saved my soul from Hell. He wrapped his loving arms around me and welcomed me into His loving eternal family. I was born again that night. I shall never forget the day the Lord Jesus Christ saved me. I received a direct reply.

Herod rejected light and didn't get one word from Jesus Christ.

Pilate--well he gets the Lord's attention but tries to stay neutral so by the end the Lord becomes silent.

The dying thief repents, and gets a straightforward, direct reply.

Chapter 4

EMMAUS ROAD

Luke 24:13 ¶ And, behold, two of them went that same day to a village called Emmaus, which was from Jerusalem about threescore furlongs.
Luke 24:14 And they talked together of all these things which had happened.
Luke 24:15 And it came to pass, that, while they communed together and reasoned, Jesus himself drew near, and went with them.
Luke 24:16 But their eyes were holden that they should not know him.
Luke 24:17 And he said unto them, What manner of communications are these that ye have one to another, as ye walk, and are sad?

Jesus, Talk To Me

With heavy hearts and confusion of mind two disciples walked the dusty dirt road on the way home Sunday afternoon. Their eyes, while staring at the road in front of them, at times teared up, and they wiped the tears away. There were periods of silence as they contemplated the events of the past three years, but especially of the past three days. Then one would break the silence with a thought, or a question only to have his friend reply, "I don't know."

Cleopas asked, "Why did they crucify Him? He didn't deserve to be crucified." Only to receive a reply from his friend of, "I don't know. It hurts to think that He is gone."

Cleopas then said, "But His body... it's not in the sepulcher, and some said they saw Him alive. Was that just their imagination? With all my heart I would like to think that He is alive, but how can that be?" He reached up and wiped some more tears away.

To this perhaps his friend replied, "I think they wanted to see Him so much that they talked themselves into it. I doubt that they saw Jesus alive. As much as I want to hear His voice again, as much as I want to listen to Him speak again, I must stay in reality, and reality is that He is gone. I will miss Him so much." They walked on in silence for a while.

This was Sunday afternoon and these two disciples were sad to think that Jesus was gone. That day there was no doubt that Herod was not

Emmaus Road

sad that Jesus was gone. If Herod even thought of Jesus Christ that day, it was only for a fleeting moment. Someone else who was not sad that day was Pilate. He had washed his hands of him, or let's say he tried to, but to him the trouble was over and resolved so let's move on with life. But on the Emmaus road that day there were two sad disciples walking home.

The soft slap of their sandals could be heard as they walked the road. The sun shone bright and the air was fresh, but their hearts were so very heavy. Then breaking the bit of silence, Cleopas speaks again saying, "I thought for sure He was the Messiah, and He was come to deliver Israel. The hope it gave me, and the joy that swelled up in me...it hurts to even think of it now. In proverbs, it says that hope deferred maketh the heart sick, and I must admit my heart is sick right now."

About that time a man walked up beside them, kind of from nowhere, and it startled them. Being pulled back into the present moment by this stranger's presence, the man then asks them, "What are you two talking about? Why are you so sad?"

With a look of incredulity they begin to tell him of all the events that have taken place over the past three days. Of course, you know from Luke 24 that it was Jesus Christ who was now walking with them, though they did not know it was Him. How He did that, I don't know, but He did.

Jesus, Talk To Me
And so He began to talk Bible with them.

> Luke 24:27 And beginning at Moses and all the prophets, he expounded unto them in all the scriptures the things concerning himself.

Oh, that must have been quite a Bible study! The more He expounded, the more their hearts leaped for joy. On and on He went, and their understanding of the scriptures grew with each new revelation. Their hearts began to burn within them as the "stranger" opened up the scriptures to them that day. All sorrow vanished away and newfound hope flooded their souls. Mile after mile, a few hours passed by, yet they seemed as mere minutes. Before they knew it, they were at the turn off to their house. Evening was setting in and it would be time for supper.

As they turned to go up the path to their house, the Lord Jesus made as though He would go further. Luke 24:28 ...he made as though he would have gone further.

You see He didn't have to go further. In other words he didn't have a pressing schedule to keep. He just made as though He would go further. Why would He do that? We are talking about the Lord of the universe here and He acted like He was going to do something that He wasn't going to do.

> John 6:5 When Jesus then lifted up his eyes, and saw a great company come unto him, he

saith unto Philip, Whence shall we buy bread, that these may eat?

John 6:6 And this he said to prove him: for he himself knew what he would do.

Here is another case in point of where the Lord put someone in a position to see what they would do.

Now, as soon as you come to this sort of subject, invariably the thought or statement comes up that the Lord knows everything, and, yes, He does. He is omniscient, which is a big theological word that means God knows everything or that He is all-knowing. Yet while that is true, there is something about reality that is not fixed into a Calvinistic sort of way, and that is man's will.

God will not step over man's free will. Even Jesus Christ had His own will that was separate from the Father, for in the Garden of Gethsemane Jesus prayed, Luke 22:42. ...not my will, but thy will be done. That is another subject we will not get into right now. Nevertheless, man has a free will and God will put people in situations at times to see what they will do. He did this with Phillip, and He did this with these two disciples on the road to Emmaus.

You may ask, what has this to do with getting God's attention? It has everything to do with getting God's attention.

They were having a great Bible study and as they came to the turn off to their house, and He made

Jesus, Talk To Me

as though He would go further. If they would have said, "We sure have enjoyed the time with you. Thank you for walking with us," then Jesus Christ would have continued on down the road for a bit and left them. Perhaps they never would have found out it was the Lord until some days later. Either way though, He was setting them up to see IF THEY WANTED HIM. You have got to get that!

When it appeared that He was going to go on down the road, Cleopas and the other disciple stopped and said in so many words, "We sure have enjoyed the conversation, and it is getting late. Well, supper is going to be ready, would you please come home with us and have supper with us?" And in so many words the Lord asks, "Do you really want me?" To which they reply, "We would count it an honor to have you come home and have supper with us. Please come to our house and abide with us." To which Jesus agreed and went in with them. They constrained Him, which means, "To compel or force (someone) toward a particular course of action." Their desire to have Him join them compelled Jesus Christ to submit to their wishes.

If you want to get the Lord's attention, then first and foremost you must repent as the dying thief did on the cross. That got the Lord's attention. Then after that, you have to want Him.

You might reply, "Oh, come on preacher, there has got to be more to it than that." Nope! That's it. And perhaps you do want Him. I am assuming at this point you have confessed your sins so I won't cover that again, but you say, "Yes I do want Him."

Well then, how does that affect your schedule? How have you gone out of your way just to spent time with Him? The Lord stands back and waits. He seems so distant from you.

For some of God's people, there was a time when the Lord Jesus Christ was right there with you, and you knew He was. You sensed His presence, prayers were answered often, and He was as real to you as your own flesh. That is what we call Bethel, and it is that place where you and God were so very, very close.

Time has passed now, and He doesn't seem to be close to you like that anymore. Something has changed and it troubles you when you think about it. Well, how much does it trouble you? He made as though He would go further. Have you constrained Him to abide with you? Does it trouble you enough to go out of your way to show Him you are serious. Psa. 42:1 As the hart panteth after the water brooks, so panteth my soul after thee, O God.

There are born again saints all over the world who at one time were very close to their Saviour, the Lord Jesus Christ. If at no other time than when they were first saved. But time has passed by and now the Lord has stepped back from them to see if they want Him, but there has been no response. They have just continued down the road of life with little to no notice that Jesus Christ is not in fellowship with them. It doesn't bother them at all.

Then there are the others who know His presence. No, it is not a feeling, but there is an awareness of His presence when He is filling you and abiding with you.

In John 15, Jesus said, "Abide in me." Where you live is called your abode because it is where you abide. Though you are not always there, yet it is where you abide. Cleopas and the other disciple contained Him saying, "Abide with us." In other words, come home with us. They desired His presence.

Does it bother you to think that the Lord's presence may be distant? Does it trouble you to the point of changing your schedule just so you can spend time with your Saviour? How is your prayer life?

I know the Bible says to pray without ceasing and there is nothing wrong with praying while you are driving, just keep your eyes open! There is nothing wrong with praying in the shower, while you are doing the dishes, etc. But there is no substitute for getting alone with Jesus Christ, shutting the world out, turning off your cell phone, (or better yet not even having it with you), finding a quiet private place, kneeling, if you can, closing your eyes and praying out loud to your Saviour. Yes, talking out loud to the One who loved you so much He died for you on the cross.

Emmaus Road

How do you get the Lord's attention? You have to want Him! Want Him to the point where it changes your daily schedule so that you can spend time alone with Him in the word of God, and on your knees privately in prayer. Repenting of your sins, and praying to Him about all--I said all, and I mean, all--of your fears, wants, hopes, and for the salvation of loved ones and friends. 1 Peter 5:7 Casting all your care upon Him, for He careth for you.

There is no doubt that He wants to spend time with you! There is no doubt that He loves you and cares for you. Do you want Him? Would you get desperate? Would you appear extreme to those around you? Would it matter to you if loved ones criticized you and laughed at you?

Maybe you are already reading and praying daily, but something doesn't seem right. If your reading and praying is mere duty, like brushing your teeth or taking a shower, then you are missing Him. Reading and praying are to times of fellowshipping with your Saviour, and if you are missing Him in your devotions, does that bother you? Are you content with doing your devotions even though they seem very dry spiritually?

Has the Lord stepped back from you waiting to see if you will notice He is gone? When you notice He is gone, does that bother you? Do you want Him, your Saviour, the Lord Jesus Christ?

We had been living on the road in the ministry of Evangelism. At this time only my wife and

Jesus, Talk To Me

daughter, Rebekah, were traveling with me in a Chevy conversion van. The road is hard and lonely since you are always moving from place to place.

One day Rebekah, who at this time was twelve years old, came to me and asked if she could pray for a dog. Now, you have got to understand that when Rebekah prayed she got her prayers answered, for she had quite a track record of answers to prayer, and how can I tell my daughter not to pray for something? I couldn't do that! I also knew that she was lonely, but a dog? A dog while living out of a car from week to week? Oh my! Well, after giving her all my concerns about it, I told her that she could pray for a dog.

I then got on my knees and prayed, "Oh, God no. Please, don't give us a dog." Well, Rebekah won and we got a dog, or I should say the Lord gave us a dog, and He did. That little dog was a blessing though, and to not only Rebekah, but to all of us. She was never a burden either. I had told Rebekah though that at times we would be a places where a dog would not be allowed in the room, such as certain motels, as well as homes we stayed in. For most of the time, all was well and "Katie" was her name, was allowed to come inside.

One meeting though, we were put up in a nice motel. It was winter, and the temperature outside was in single digits at night. Rebekah was almost in tears, for they would not allow dogs inside the motel. We had let Katie grow her hair very long, she was a Shih Tzu, so that helped, and then we piled down pillows all around and over her to keep her warm at night. We even got a Coleman propane heater to put in the van, but it wouldn't burn all night long.

That night Rebekah had a hard time sleeping. It was very cold. In the morning we got ready to go. Coming out to the van, I opened the door, and from under the pillows little Katie poked her head out. Rebekah reached for her, and Katie leaped into her arms just a wiggling and shaking with excitement.

As Rebekah held her, Katie was squealin' and licking Rebekah's cheeks. Katie was so excited to see Rebekah! Rebekah excitedly kept saying, "oh Katie, oh Katie, oh Katie!" I could tell that Rebekah's heart was melting.

Katie was saying in dog language, "I love you, oh, I missed you so much, it is so good to see you."

Then Terri took her and as Katie was licking her face Terri was saying, "oh Katie, oh Katie, oh Katie." I could also tell that Terri's heart was melting.

Upon observing this whole scene, then I took Katie and began to say, "oh Katie, oh Katie, oh Katie." Did my heart melt? Well...maybe a little.

Do you know why all three of us wanted to hold Katie? Because she wanted us to, and was excited to see us.

There were other times when we would come out to the van, unlock the door and Katie would merely look up from her bed and then lay her head back down. When she did that, guess what? We didn't

Jesus, Talk To Me

pick her up, nor did we pay any attention to her. Why? She didn't care if we did or didn't!

How do you get God's attention? You have to want Him. If it has been a while since He has been close, does that bother you? To the point of not hungry? To the point of losing sleep?

He made as though He would go further, why?

Do you want Me?

Let me leave you with one more thought. When time is no more and this universe has melted with fervent heat, do you know who is going to be in Heaven? All who chose to be there. They were not forced, they chose Jesus Christ because they wanted to.

Do you want the Lord Jesus Christ to abide with you?

www.ingramcontent.com/pod-product-compliance
Lightning Source LLC
Chambersburg PA
CBHW071756080526
44588CB00013B/2263